# The Little Book of Qig
Chinese Exercises for the si healthy.

**By Ken Ward**

Copyright © 2017 Ken Ward

# Contents

Contents ............................................................................. 3
Introduction ....................................................................... 6
What are the Benefits of the Exercises? ..................................... 8
Who can Practice? .............................................................. 10
How Accurately Should I Assume the Postures ......................... 11
Smile, When You Practise ................................................... 12
How Should I Practise Fast or Slow? ..................................... 13
Breathing .......................................................................... 14
The Initial Position ............................................................. 15
Eight Brocade, First Posture ................................................ 19
    Reaching up to the sky ................................................... 20
    Position 1 .................................................................... 21
    Position 2 .................................................................... 22
    Position 3 .................................................................... 23
    Sequence Reaching up to the Sky ................................... 24
Second Posture, Drawing the Bow ........................................ 25
    Position 1 .................................................................... 26
    Position 2 .................................................................... 28
    Position 3 .................................................................... 29
    Position 4 .................................................................... 30
    Sequence, Drawing the Bow ........................................... 31
Third Posture: Raise Each Arm ............................................ 32
    Position 1 .................................................................... 33
    Position 2 .................................................................... 34
    Position 3 .................................................................... 35

- Position 4 .................................................................................. 36
- Position 5 .................................................................................. 37
- Position 6 .................................................................................. 38
- Position 7 .................................................................................. 39
- Sequence: Third Posture: Raise Each Arm ............................... 40
- Fourth Set: Looking Behind ............................................................ 41
  - Position 1 .................................................................................. 42
  - Position 2 .................................................................................. 43
  - Position 3 .................................................................................. 44
- Sequence: Looking Behind .............................................................. 46
- Qigong Set Five: Bending Over and Wagging the Tail .................. 47
  - Position 1 .................................................................................. 48
  - Position 2 .................................................................................. 49
  - Position 3 .................................................................................. 50
  - Sequence: Bending Over and Wagging the Tail .................... 51
- Sixth Set: Reaching Down ............................................................... 52
  - Position 1 .................................................................................. 53
  - Position 2 .................................................................................. 54
  - Sequence: Reaching Down ..................................................... 55
- Seventh Set: Punching with Angry Gaze ........................................ 56
  - Position 1 .................................................................................. 57
  - Position 2 .................................................................................. 58
  - Position 3 .................................................................................. 59
  - Sequence: Punching with Angry Gaze .................................. 60
- Eighth Set: Touch the Toes ............................................................. 61
  - Position 1 .................................................................................. 62
  - Position 2 .................................................................................. 63
  - Sequence: Touch the Toes ...................................................... 64

Summary of the Sets ................................................................ 65
　1 Reaching for the Sky.......................................................... 66
　2 Drawing the Bow .............................................................. 67
　3 Raise Each Arm ................................................................ 68
　4 Looking Behind ................................................................ 69
　5 Bending Over and Wagging the Tail ............................... 70
　6 Reaching Down................................................................ 71
　7 Punching With Angry Gaze .............................................. 72
　8 Touch the Toes.................................................................. 73

# Introduction

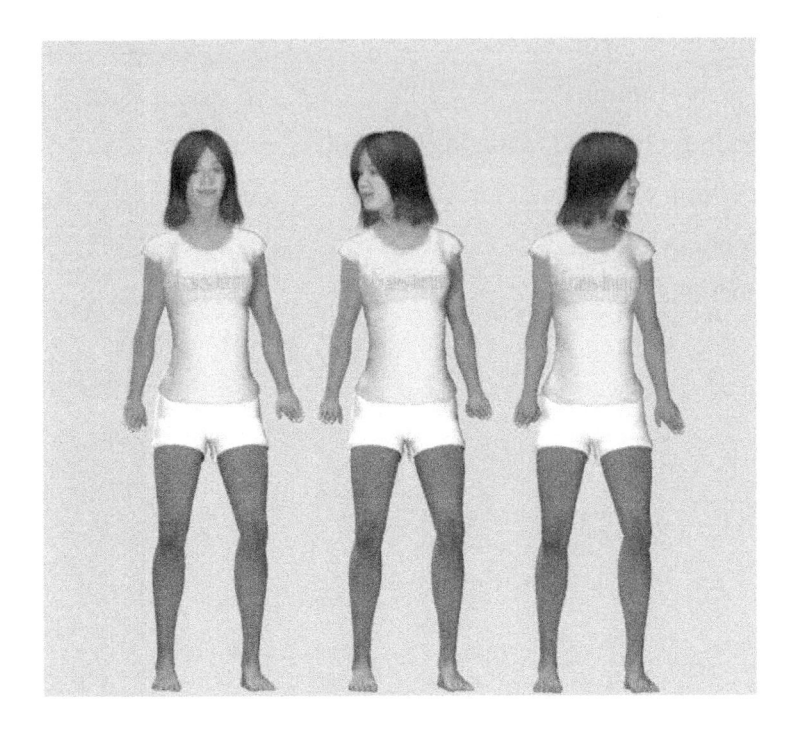

This is a short book giving the essentials of Qigong practice.

There are thousands of postures in qigong, and various styles. The postures shown here are not the only ones. These first exercises are called the "Eight Brocade" and can be very easy physically. They can, however, be practised enthusiastically and energetically, but in this book, the gentle way is emphasised.

In particular, as we learn from our practice, we allow ourselves to be aware of our breathing and body sensations. This is why these pages are concerned with postures from qigong (although any postures might serve as well). When we move our bodies with awareness, we experience tensions in our bodies, and have the opportunity to observe our reactions to these sensations. That is, we can do the exercises mindfully.

Also we emphasise personal exploration of experience in the now. In practising we allow ourselves to place our attention on the now, but we do not attempt to change anything. We allow what is, to be.

*"All things spring up, and there is not one which declines to show itself; they grow, and there is no claim made for their ownership; they go through their processes, and there is no expectation (of a reward for the results)."* Lao Tsu

# What are the Benefits of the Exercises?

None at all. It is not so much as what you might attain, but what you might give up that impedes your being– for instance– truly happy.

*"All things spring up, and there is not one which declines to show itself; they grow, and there is no claim made for their ownership; they go through their processes, and there is no expectation (of a reward for the results)."* Lao Tsu

In learning about your mind and your body through mindfulness, you become your own guide. Where you guide yourself, depends on you.

The suggested principals of meditation are those of giving up:

- judging;
- impatience;
- 'knowing' without first experiencing;
- distrust and suspicion;
- striving; wishing what is, were not; and
- hanging on to past pain and suffering.

The seven principles, according to Jon Kabbat-Zin are:

1. Non-judging
2. Patience
3. Beginners Mind
4. Trust
5. Non-striving
6. Acceptance
7. Letting go

It is OK to be judgmental, impatient, etc, but we try to recognise mindfully when we are like this, or, more accurately, we recognise when these thoughts arise in our minds, and recognise the bodily sensations that relate to these.

In the present moment there is only what is, therefore there can be no attainment in that moment.

*"Therefore the sage puts his own person last, and yet it is found in the foremost place;*
*he treats his person as if it were foreign to him, and yet that person is preserved.*
*Is it not because he has no personal and private ends, that therefore such ends are realised?"* – Lao Tsu

# Who can Practice?

I assume anyone who practises these postures and the meditation is in normal mental and physical health. If you have any doubts, consult someone who can advise you, such as your health provider.

In China, qigong is used as a therapy, and people can practise standing, sitting, or lying on a bed. They are, of course, under the supervision of their health care provider, and are often taught the movements by a doctor.

If you cannot stand, do the exercises sitting. If you cannot sit, do the exercises lying. If you cannot move, do the exercises mentally.

# How Accurately Should I Assume the Postures

"*there are first the sprouts; then perfection. First, there is perversion; then rectification. First there is hollowness [receptivity]; then plenitude. First there is destruction [of the old]; then renovation. First there is humility; then acquisition.*" —Lao Tsu

For the purposes of meditation, the postures are not that important (at first), although they are well-thought of, apparently, in China. While we are being kind to ourselves we do not seek perfection, only to observe mindfully as we practice, and by extension, to observe mindfully as we live our lives.

# Smile, When You Practise

Where possible, and we all forget sometimes, smile when you practise!

At least move your mouth into a smiling shape ☺

However, in some poses, you should make an angry face, when instructed.

# How Should I Practise Fast or Slow?

The emphasis is on meditation, so the postures are assumed slowly, perhaps very slowly.

When the arms are extended, the joints are not locked, but kept loose.

Movements are made, where appropriate, in a circular manner rather than in straight lines.

At least, start gently, but you might speed up as you learn.

# Breathing

Breathe naturally and easily, without force or effort. Even in traditional qigong different people use different breathing patterns. Discover what is best for you, in a gentle and easy manner.

In general, when reaching upwards or outwards (opening the chest) you might want to breathe in. And when reaching downwards, you might want to breathe out. At the extreme position, if you pause, then breathe naturally.

# The Initial Position

The initial position is simply standing in a natural posture, with the legs slightly bent and the arms hanging loosely at the sides. The unfocussed eyes may look a few feet ahead of you.

All the sets or postures begin and end in this position, shown below:

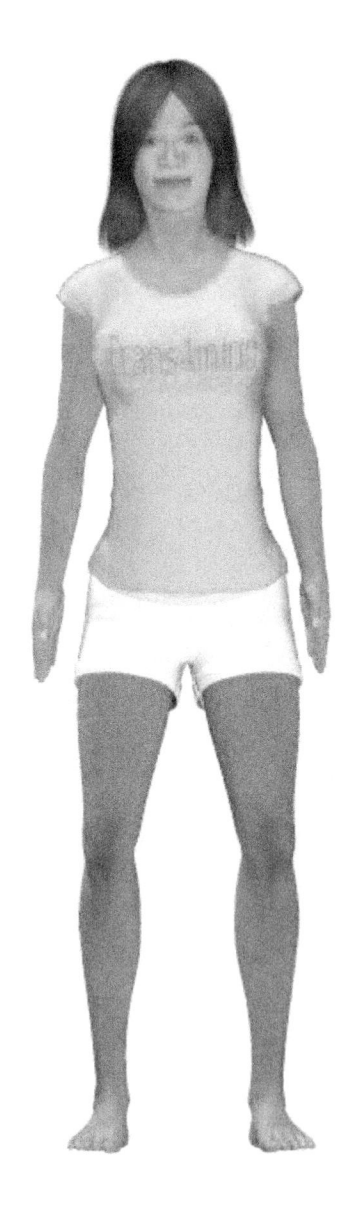

Put your attention on your breathing, perhaps your abdominal breathing, noting the rise and fall of the stomach as you breathe.

Allow yourself to breathe, and simply be aware of your breathing. You allow your breaths to be as they come, deep or shallow. Just observe the breath.

Your feet may be flat on the floor and you can put your awareness on the sensations in your feet as they support the body. Feel how the feet are grounded on the floor (or ground) in an easy and relaxed manner.

Stand simply in a relaxed manner, with your attention on your breathing, observing and allowing it to be.

If you drift into daydreaming, thinking, or storytelling, note this, and gently return your awareness to your breathing.

If you feel the compulsion to do something else, or to move, see if you can note the feeling or sensation in your body and perhaps the impulse to move compulsively.

Perhaps you feel bored and must do something else. Let this body feeling or sensation be, and note what it is like. And if you absolutely must do something else, perhaps the next posture, or make a cup of coffee, or telephone someone, allow this feeling to occur and see if you can wait, just observing in the now, and see what happens next (usually nothing). You may notice how this feeling reaches a maximum and then declines. Of course, you are attending to bodily feelings, not to thoughts. Everyone can wait a few seconds, and if you decide to move or do something else, then do so with awareness and as a conscious decision, rather than as a mindless automatic action. It is OK to decide to move on and do something else.

You may decide to spend a few minutes (or longer) in this position, having your awareness in present time, attending mainly to your breathing.

Note any bodily sensations, any thoughts or images that arise in the mind, perhaps acknowledging them, with the thought (label),

"Thought arising", "Image arising" and return to concentrating on your breathing.

With practice you may be aware of the whole body, just standing there breathing and any sounds occurring in the environment.

# Eight Brocade, First Posture

## *Reaching up to the sky*

Begin and end the sequence in the Initial Position, shown below:

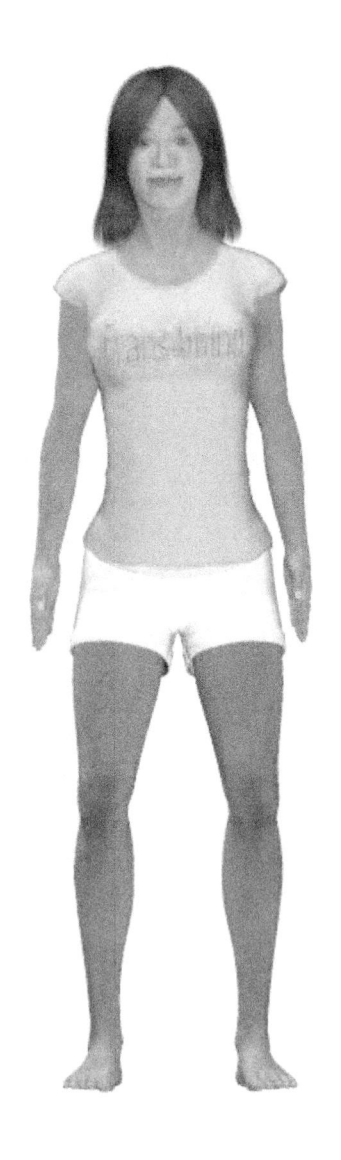

## *Position 1*

From the initial posture, slowly raising the arms in a circular manner and place the hands on the head, **palms down**.

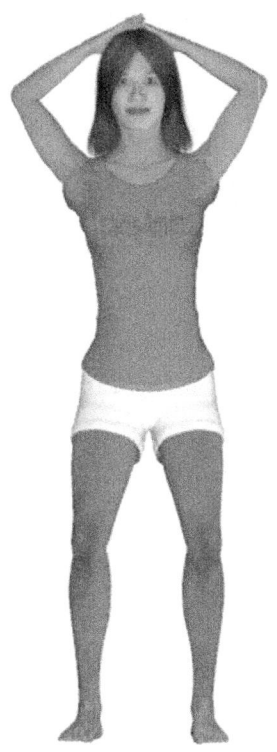

As you raise your arms be aware of the sensations in your arms. If you notice tension, pause in the movement to put your awareness on the tension. With practice, you might notice as you pause, an impulse to move to a more comfortable position. If possible, wait a second or two to note what happens. When you continue, do so deliberately, having made a conscious decision to continue the movement.

As you pause in this position, be aware of your breathing, of the rising and falling of the stomach as you breathe. Breathe naturally, allowing your breathing to be as it is, and allow your awareness to be in present time.

## *Position 2*

Mindfully **raise** your arms above your head with the **palms still down**. You can also **stand tiptoe**, if you are able. Pause for a while in this position noting your bodily sensations. If you feel an impulse to move be aware of this, and wait a few seconds to see what happens, perhaps the rising and falling away of the tension.

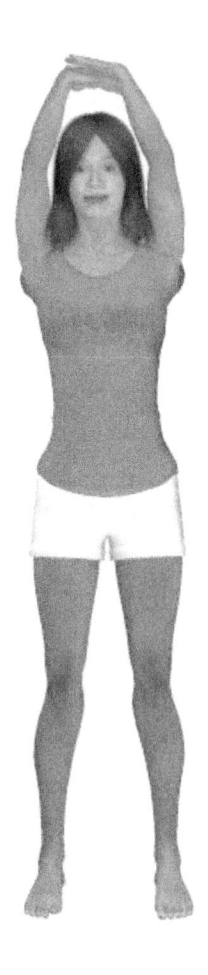

Consciously decide to move your arms down so your palms rest on your head, and your feet flat on the floor (if you stood tiptoe).

Pause for a while being aware of your breathing.

## *Position 3*

Raise your arms above your head: this time **turning your hands so the palms face upwards**. Be mindful of your breathing and your body and any sensations as you pause.

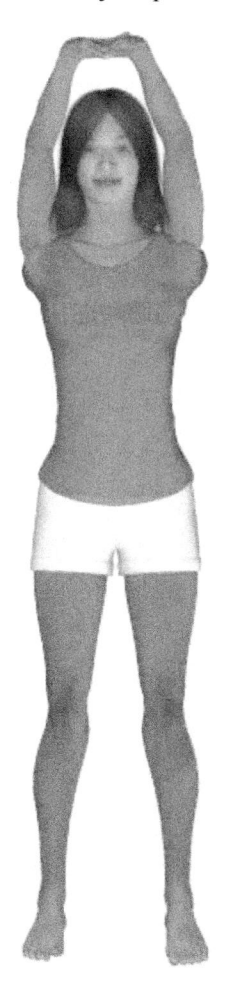

Bring your arms down to rest on your head, **palms still facing upwards** and pause awhile. This hand position is the opposite of that in Position 1.

Bring your arms up again, turning the hands so the palms face downwards, as in the second movement above.

## *Sequence Reaching up to the Sky*

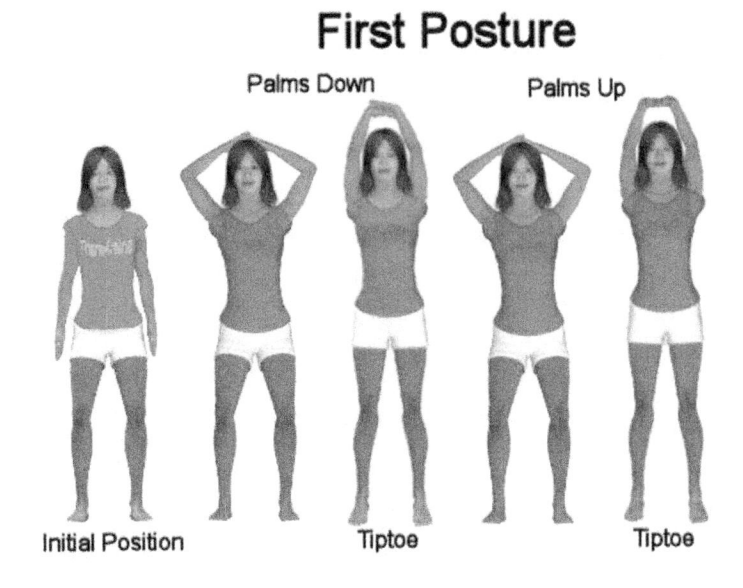

### First Posture

Palms Down       Palms Up

Initial Position      Tiptoe      Tiptoe

Repeat the sequence two or three times, or more as you progress.

# Second Posture, Drawing the Bow

This posture is called drawing the bow and is based on the observation of archers and how they developed certain parts of their bodies.

Begin and end the sequence in the Initial Position:

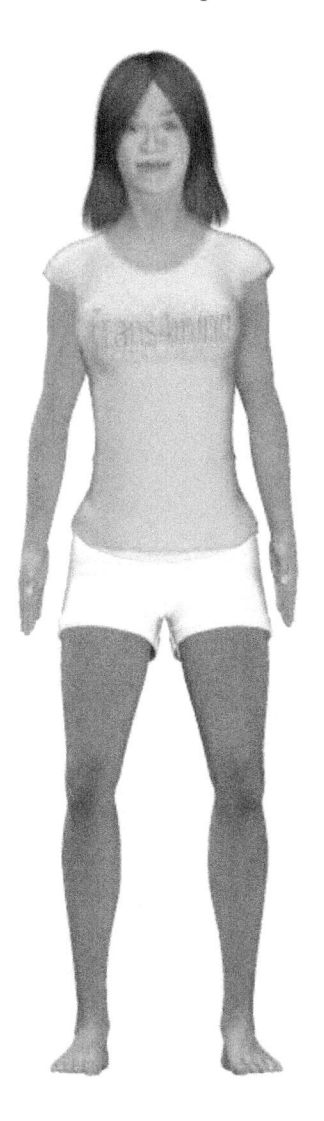

## *Position 1*

Begin in the initial position, and start this posture in a horse-riding stance, with the legs three-feet apart and slightly (or more) bent. Circle the arms round so the hands, in fists and back to back, as in the close up below.

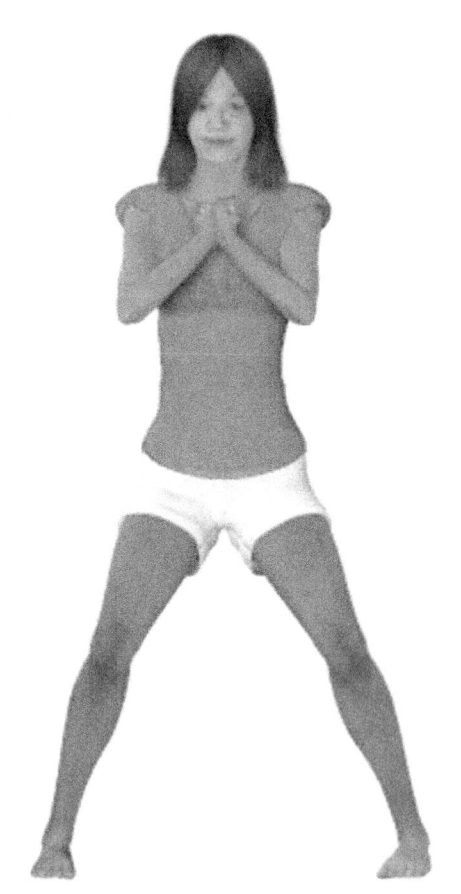

Pause for a while, being mindful of your breathing, of the rising and falling of the stomach as you breathe naturally, allowing the breath to be as it likes, deep or shallow. Just observe it.

As you become more practiced, you can be aware of the tensions in the body, in the legs and in the arms.

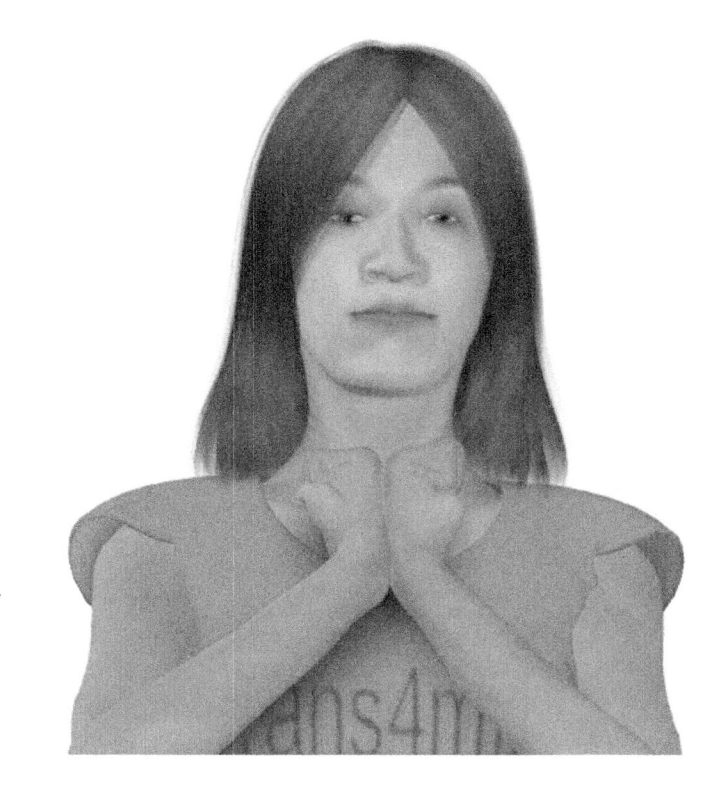

The close up above shows the starting hand position for the next position, below.

## *Position 2*

Circle the right arm out so it is extended to the right, the gaze on the hand or straight ahead. At the same time, the left hand is drawn back in a fist, the hand circling so the back of the hand is outward. The right arm is gently extended, and the joints are relaxed, not locked. The right hand can be a loose fist, or somewhat open with the first two fingers bent out, as in the picture.

As usual pause in the extreme position, being mindful of your body, breathing, in that position, and mindful of the bodily sensations of tension in the muscles.
The right hand can be in a tight fist, or a loose one, as in the pictures.

## *Position 3*
Circle the arms and hands downwards back to the starting position for this posture, repeated below.

## *Position 4*

Here, you perform the punch or stretch, with the left hand extended. It is the mirror image of Position 2.
Extend the left arm circling the hand and drawing back the right arm, as a mirror image of the previous bow posture.

## *Sequence, Drawing the Bow*
### Set 2 Sequence

Repeat the sequence two or three times, or more as you progress.

# Third Posture: Raise Each Arm

Begin and end the posture in the Initial Position. Shown also below:

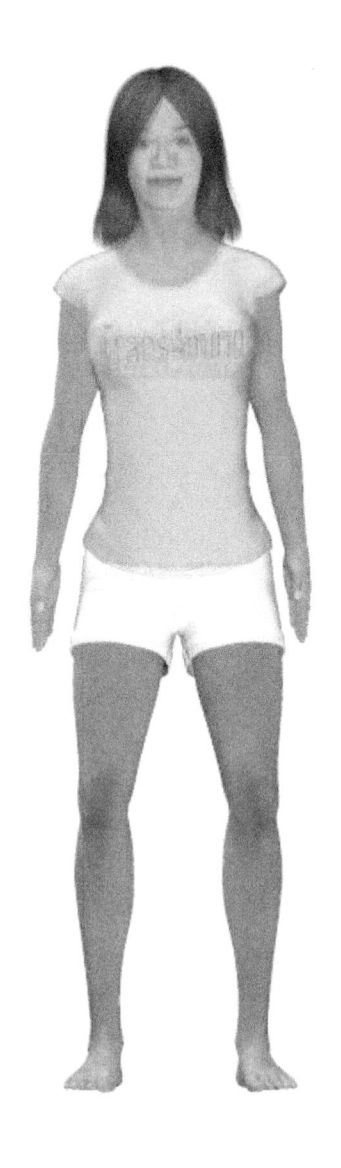

## *Position 1*

At the start, the two hands are by the sides and the palms of the hands are facing downwards. The thumbs are closest to the body.

You may press down in this position against an imaginary force.

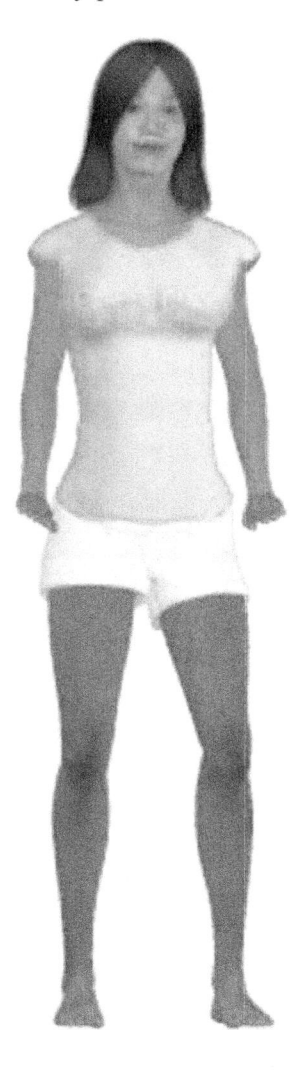

## *Position 2*

Raise the right arm so it rests on the crown of the head with the palm upwards. You may wish to pause at this point to mindfully explore the sensations and muscle tension in the body.

Note, as in all the steps, any tendency to automatically move to the next position. If you notice this automatic tendency or actual movement, see if you can wait a few seconds and observe what happens next when you do not respond to the compulsion to move. Consciously, when you decide, continue to the next step.

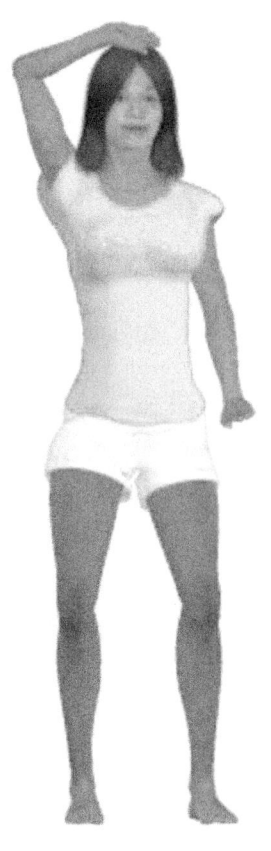

Pause and explore the sensations in the body, in particular the stretching of the chest and the shoulders.

## *Position 3*

After pausing and exploring with an open mind, raise the right arm, pushing upwards against an imaginary force and pushing downwards with the left hand against another imaginary force.

Pause and explore the sensations in the body, in particular the stretching of the chest and the shoulders.

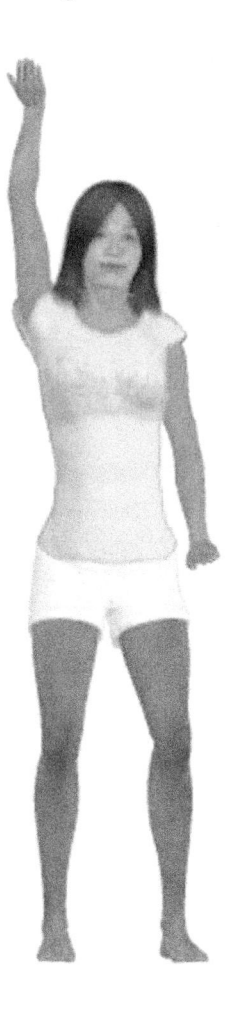

## *Position 4*
Bring the right hand down so you are in the starting position again. Pause as you wish to explore sensations, relief from tension, etc.
Both hands press down against imaginary forces.

## *Position 5*
Begin the cycle again with the left hand raising to the crown of the head, **palm up**. Notice the tension of twisting the hand, in particular, and any other sensations.

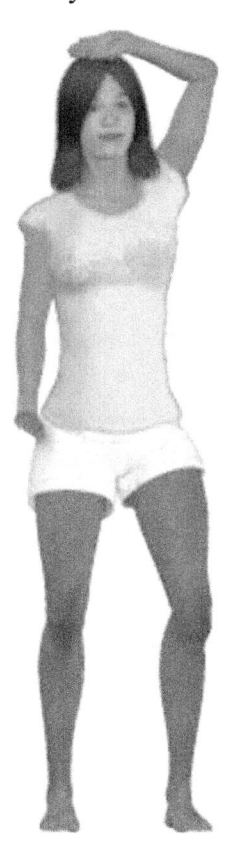

## *Position 6*

Raise your left arm upwards, **palm facing upwards**, and the two hands pushing up (left hand) and pushing down (right hand) against imaginary forces. As before pause to experience the tensions in the muscles, chest, shoulders, etc.

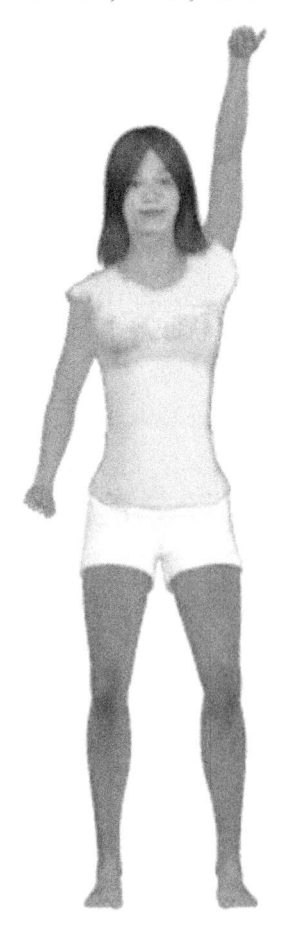

## *Position 7*

When you decide, move your arm down to the starting position (picture below). Pause a while to experience mindfully the sensations in the body, perhaps relief from the tension of stretching up.

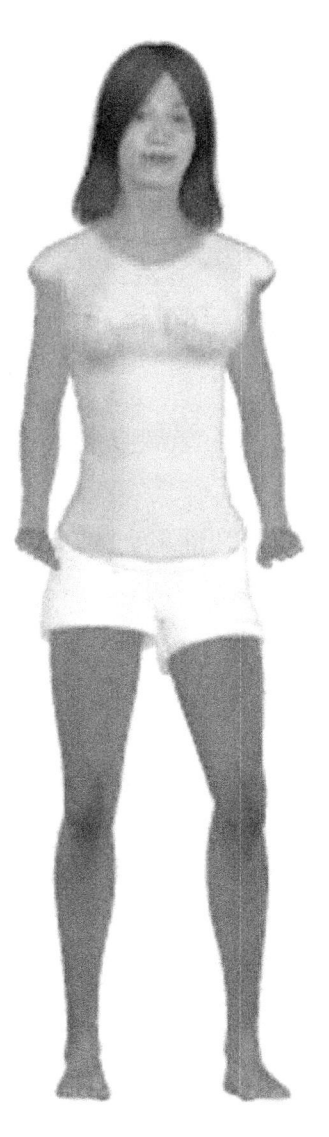

## *Sequence: Third Posture: Raise Each Arm*

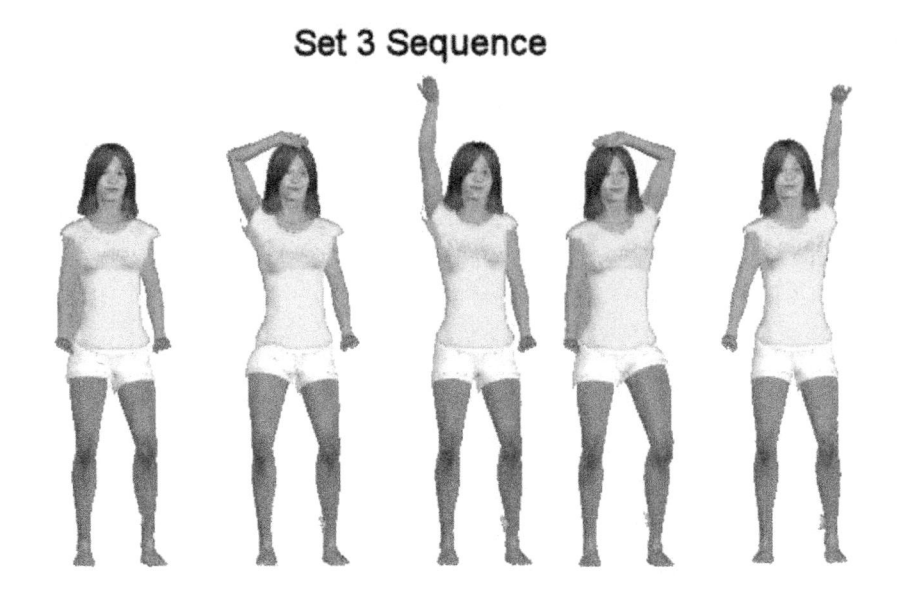

**Set 3 Sequence**

Repeat the sequence two or three times, or more as you progress.

# Fourth Set: Looking Behind

As always, begin and end in the Initial Position, shown below:

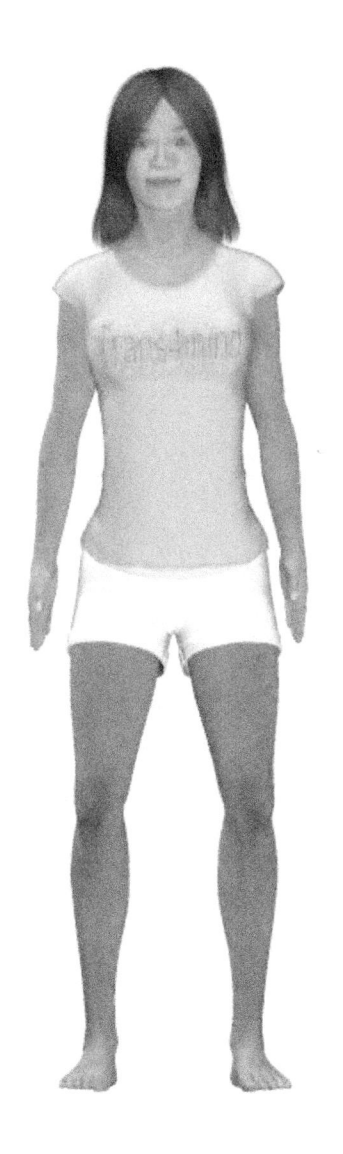

## *Position 1*

Begin from the third set, in the final position, hands pressing down on an imaginary force.

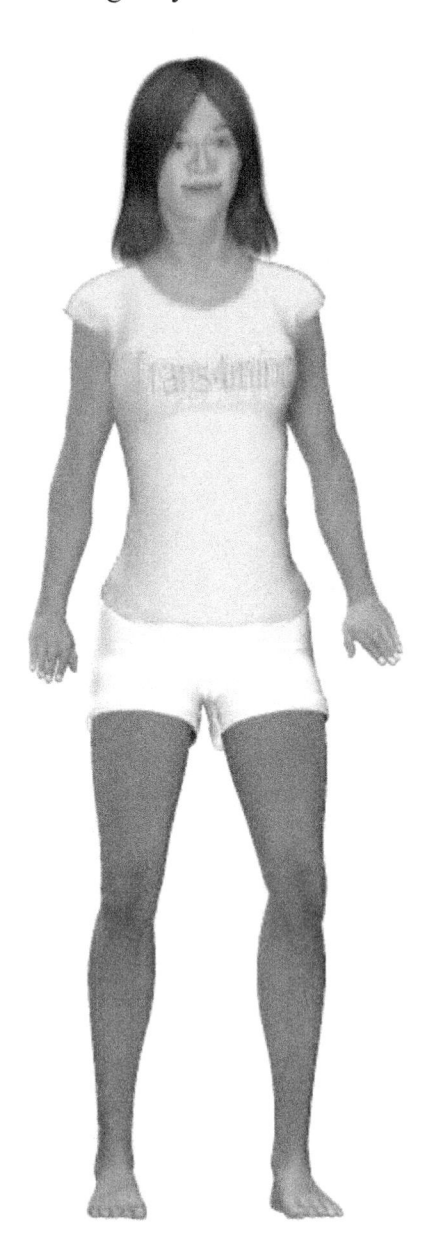

## *Position 2*

Turn the head to the right as far as it is comfortable to do so. As usual, be mindful, experiencing the moment.

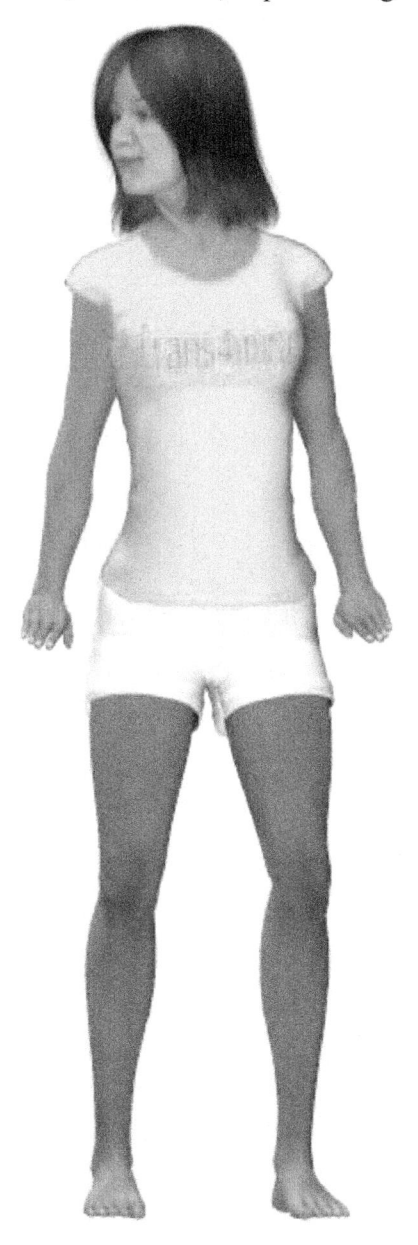

## *Position 3*
When you are ready, consciously decide to turn the head to the left, and experience this position.

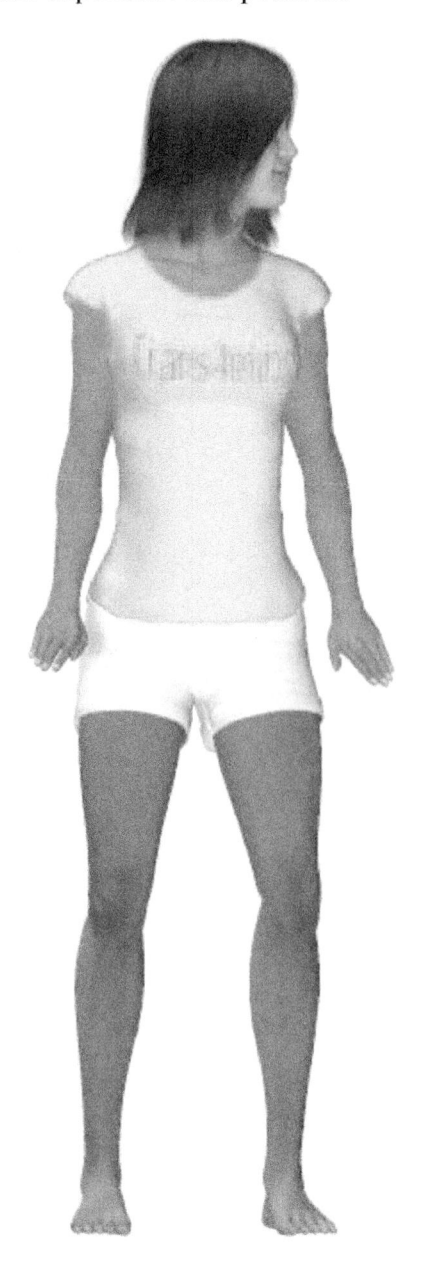

Repeat the set three or more times.

# Sequence: Looking Behind

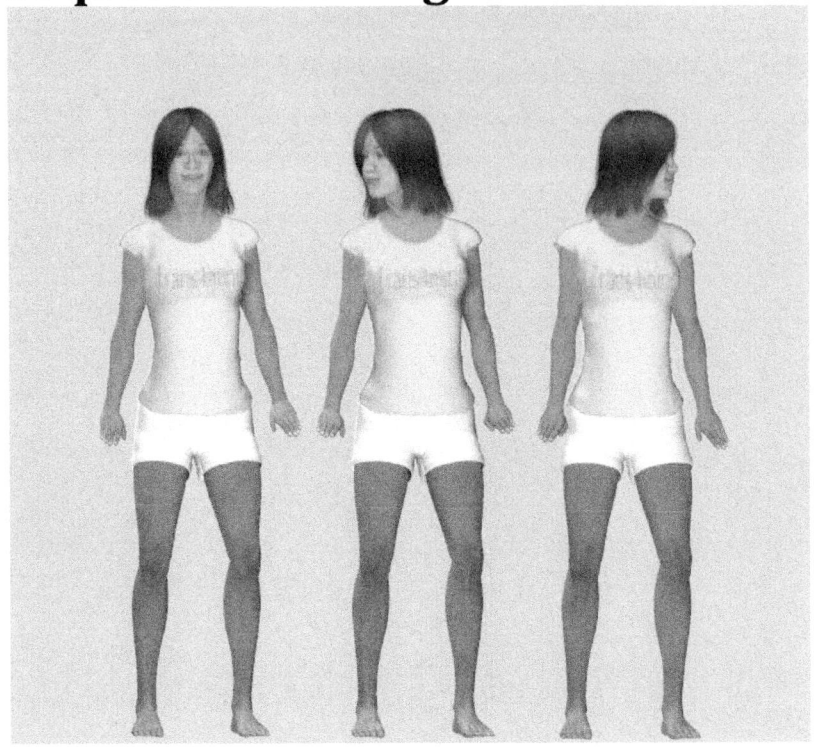

Repeat the sequence two or three times, or more as you progress.

# Qigong Set Five: Bending Over and Wagging the Tail

Begin and end in the Initial Position, shown below:

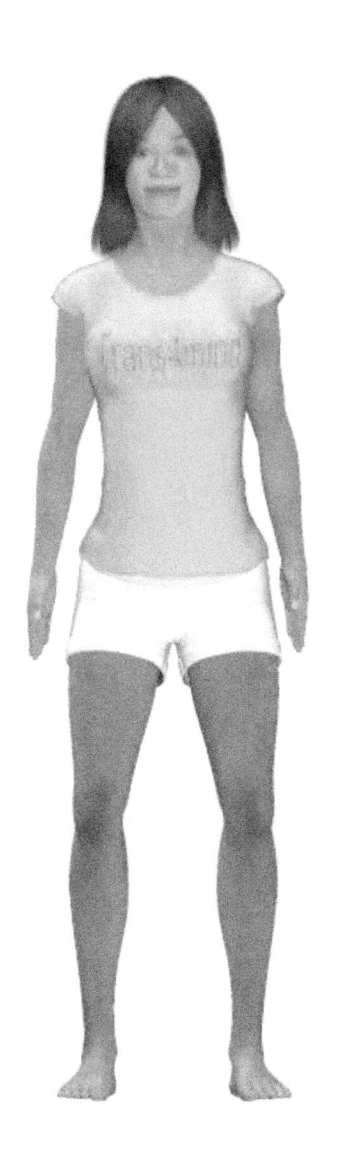

## *Position 1*

Stand in a horse-riding stance, as is comfortable for you, breathing easily and taking a moment to pause and be mindful of your abdomen rising and falling. The gaze should be a focused loosely a few feet ahead, looking down. The hands are on the hips and the spine straight.

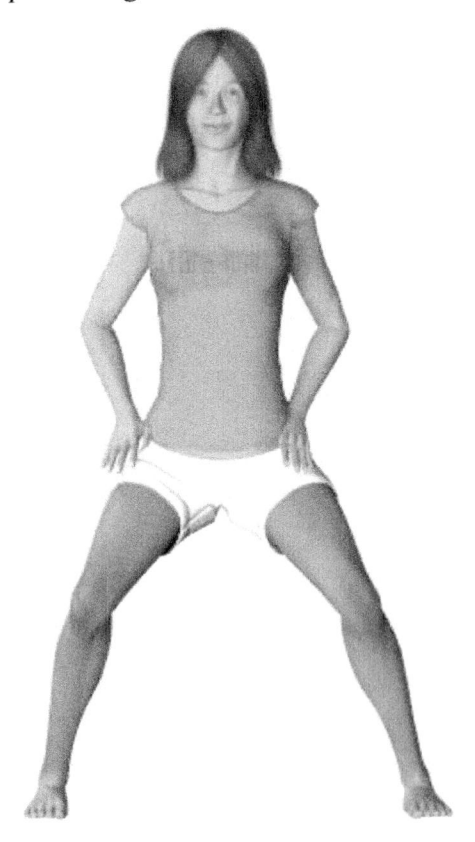

## *Position 2*

As is comfortable, slowly roll the body to the right in a circle. Circle around to the left as far as is comfortable, being aware of the body sensations. And in a circular manner, move back to the starting position.

## Position 3
Repeat the same actions to the other side, that is beginning by bending to the left, move down in a circular manner and bend to the right and back to the starting position.

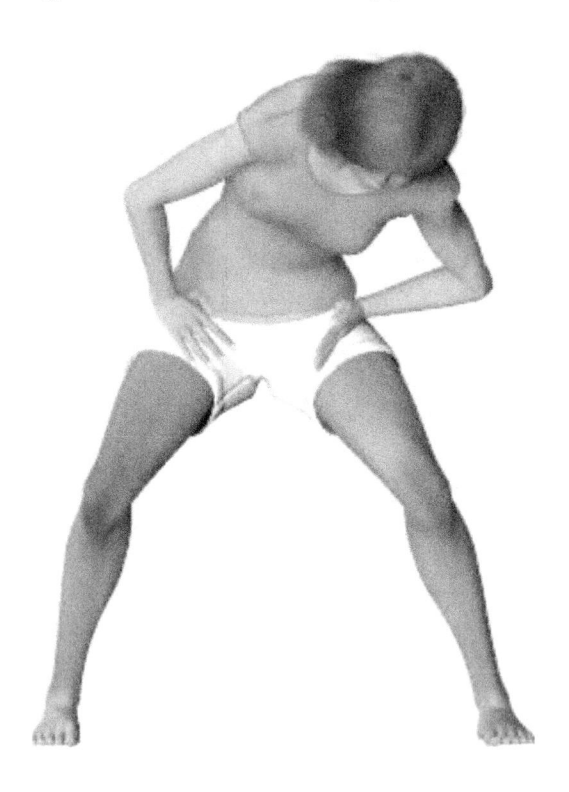

## *Sequence: Bending Over and Wagging the Tail*

Set 5 Sequence

Repeat the sequence two or three times, or more as you progress.

# Sixth Set: Reaching Down

As usual, begin in the initial position.

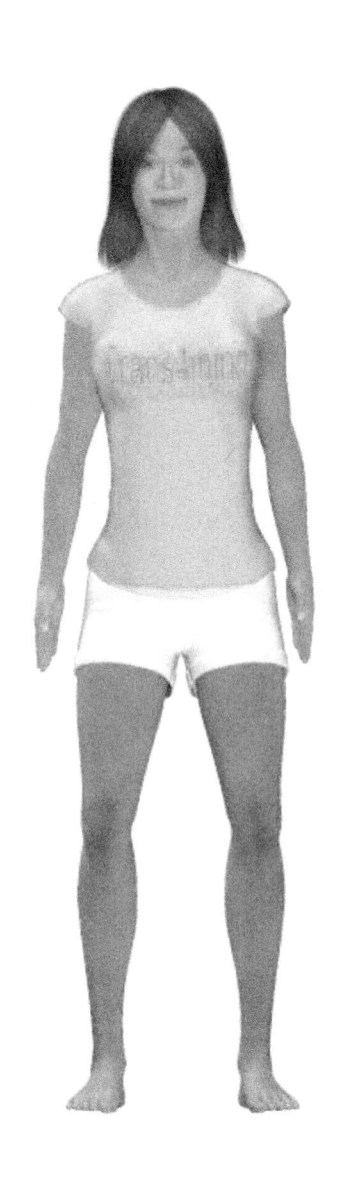

## *Position 1*
Standing easily in a relaxed manner with the hands on the buttocks, and the knees slightly bent.

54

## *Position 2*

Bend down and let the hands slip down the backs of the legs. Do this slowly and easily, as you are able.

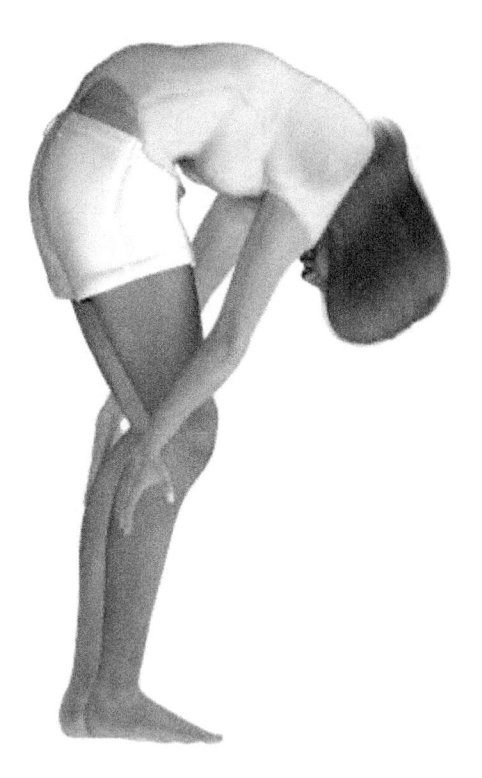

Slowly return to the starting position, stroking the backs of the legs.

## *Sequence: Reaching Down*

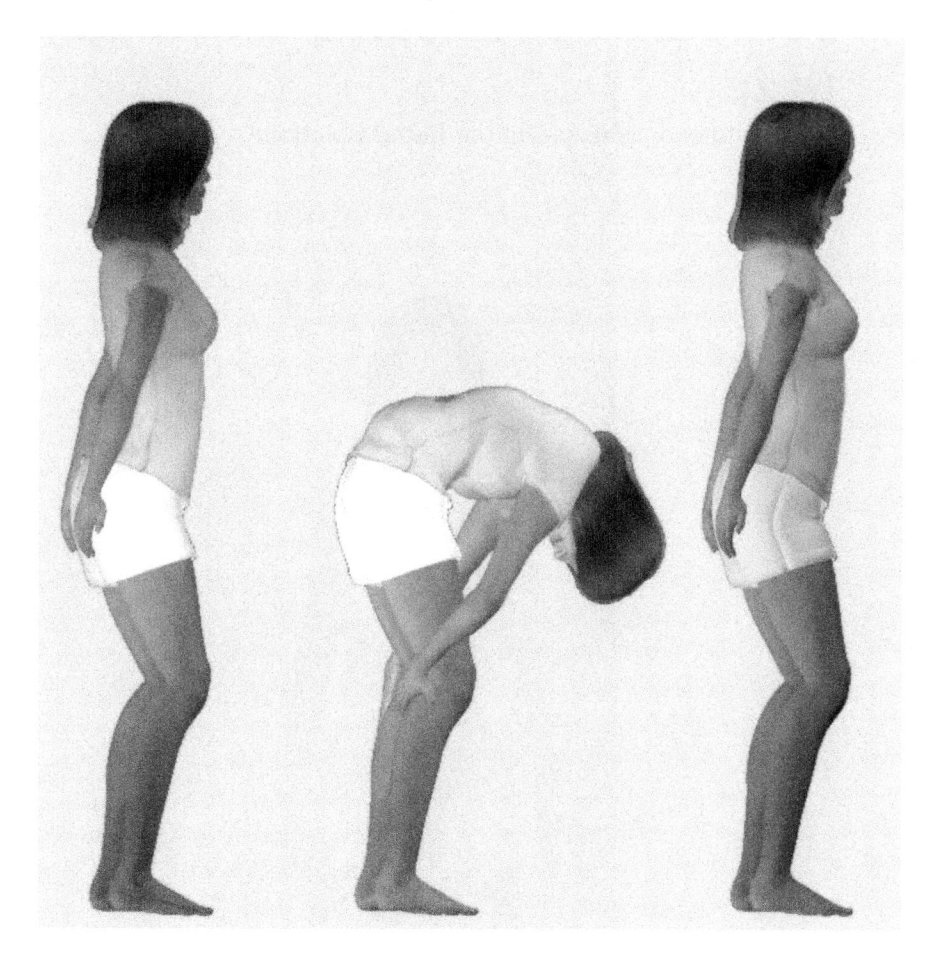

Repeat the sequence two or three times, or more as you progress.

# Seventh Set: Punching with Angry Gaze

Begin and end, as usual, in the Initial Position:

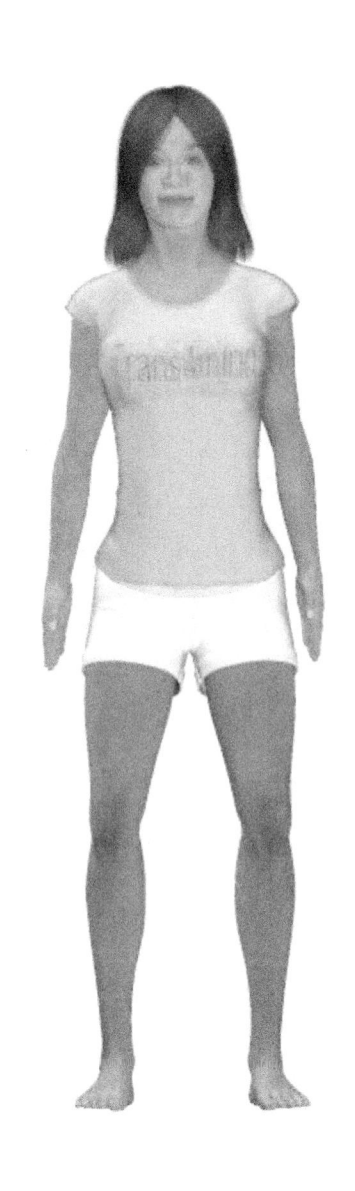

## *Position 1*

This is a somewhat controversial set. On this page, the set is performed in a traditional manner. Feel anger and 'make a face like tiger', staring ahead. The legs are in a horse-riding stance, about 3 feet apart and the fists clenched, palms upwards. Sometimes people think they have an anger problem, and sometimes they think they are never angry. Here we might become aware of anger and therefore be more able to recognise it.

One point is that even the most angry person, trying to maintain her anger, would soon find that like all things, anger might arise, we observe it mindfully, without trying to influence it. And then it declines. And we notice how it goes away.

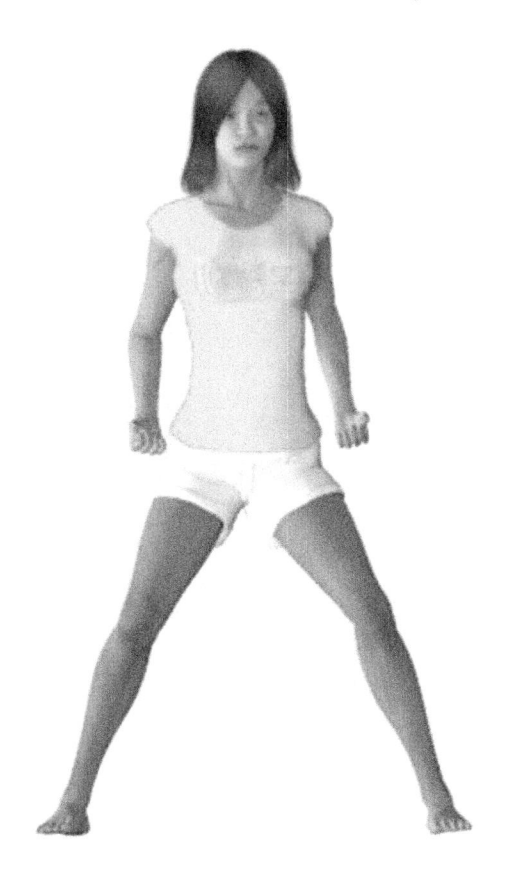

## *Position 2*

From the starting position, we reach out with the right hand, twisting the fist so it ends up with the palm down. The left hand is withdrawn, producing, with the right fist a twisting action in the body. The joints are never locked in qigong (or in the Eastern martial arts), so the right arm isn't wholly straight.

Pause at the extreme to be mindful.

## *Position 3*

Withdraw the right arm slowly, twisting so the fist ends up palm upwards, while the left arm is extended and the left fist is turned so it ends up with palm facing downwards.

## *Sequence: Punching with Angry Gaze*

Repeat the sequence two or three times, or more as you progress.

# Eighth Set: Touch the Toes

## Initial Position
Particularly with this exercise, we keep in mind that while some people can touch their toes, even after some practice, some people never can – because of their anatomy. So, this exercise, as with all the sets, is practiced easily, without striving, or attempting too much too soon. You reach down as far as you comfortably can.

Begin, as usual, in the initial position, with the legs slightly bent and the arms hanging by the side in a relaxed and easy manner. The gaze looking in an unfocussed manner about three feet ahead.

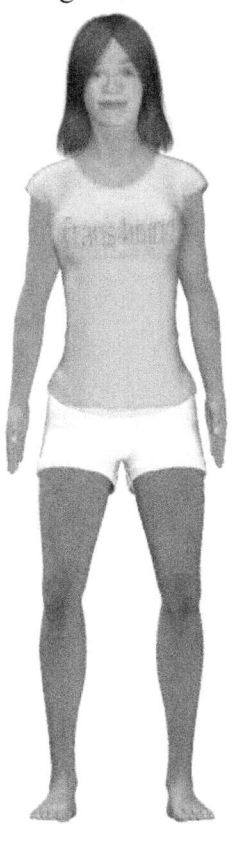

## *Position 1*

Slowly and easily, bend forwards, bringing the hands down towards the toes. As mentioned, some people cannot touch their toes, even after practice. Go down as far as it is easy for you to go.

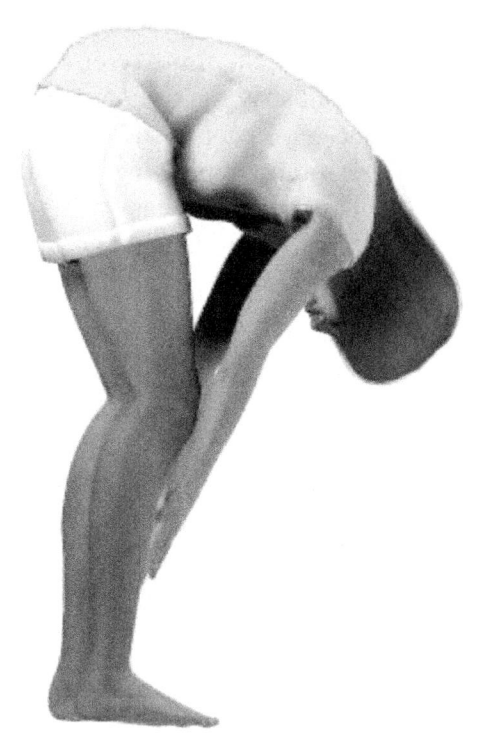

After practising for a while, some can put their hands flat on the ground, but this also depends on their anatomy. However far you can reach is fine. Do not push yourself.

## *Position 2*
Then after pausing with mindful awareness of the body, slowly return to the upward position and bend backwards as is comfortable.

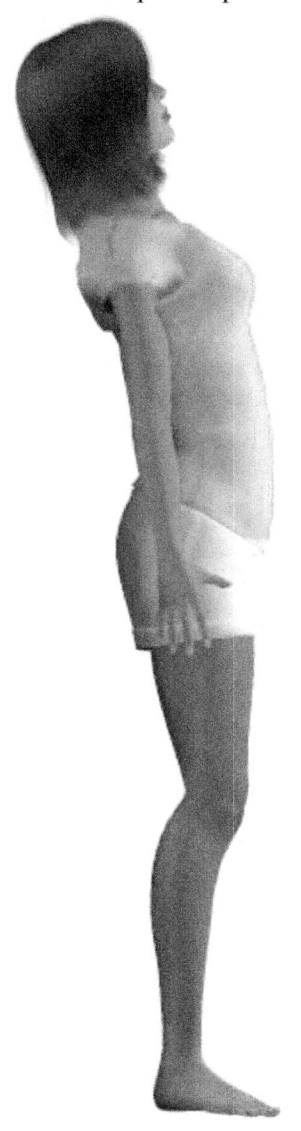

## *Sequence: Touch the Toes*

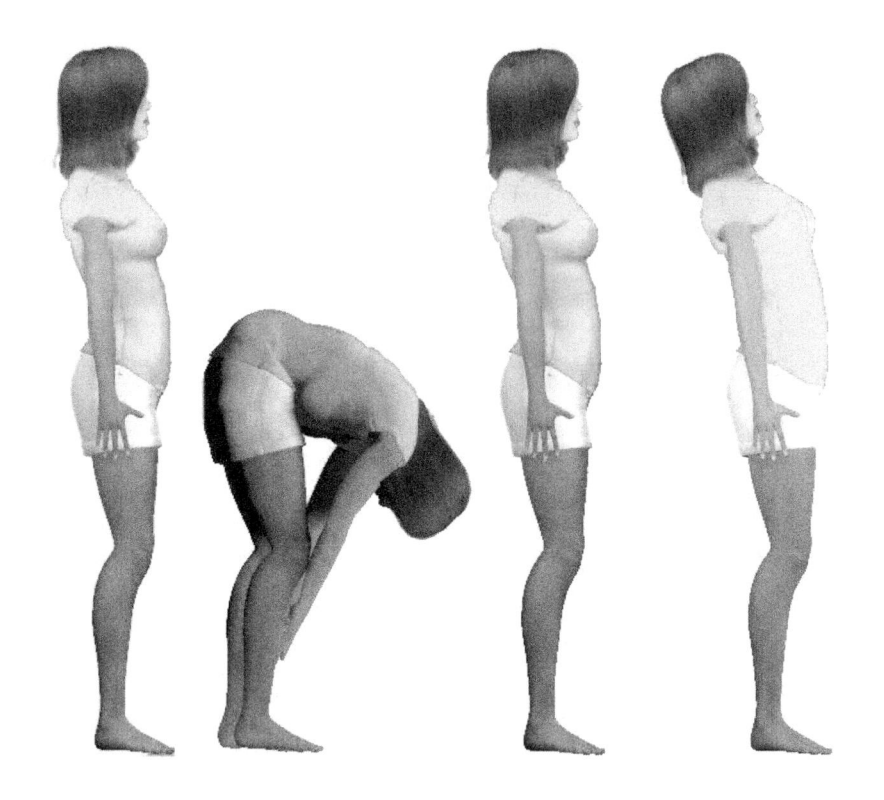

Repeat the sequence two or three times, or more as you progress.

# Summary of the Sets
## Initial Position
All of the sets or sequences begin and end in the initial position, shown below. Stand with the knees slightly bent and the arms hanging by the side in a relaxed and easy manner. The gaze should be in an unfocussed manner on a point about three feet ahead.

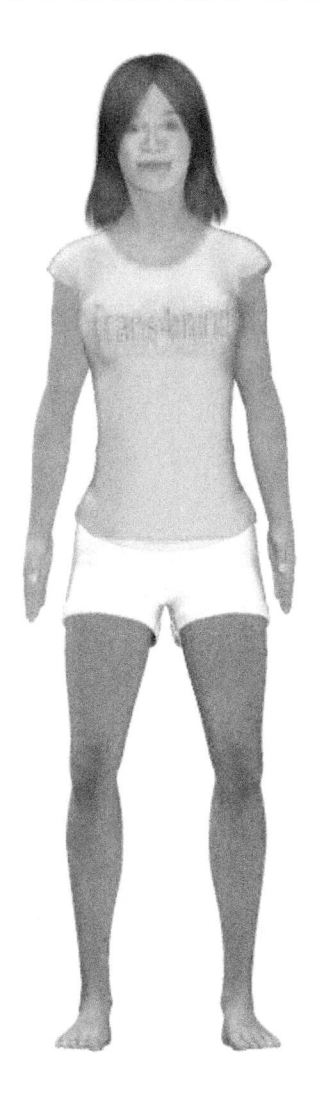

## *1 Reaching for the Sky*

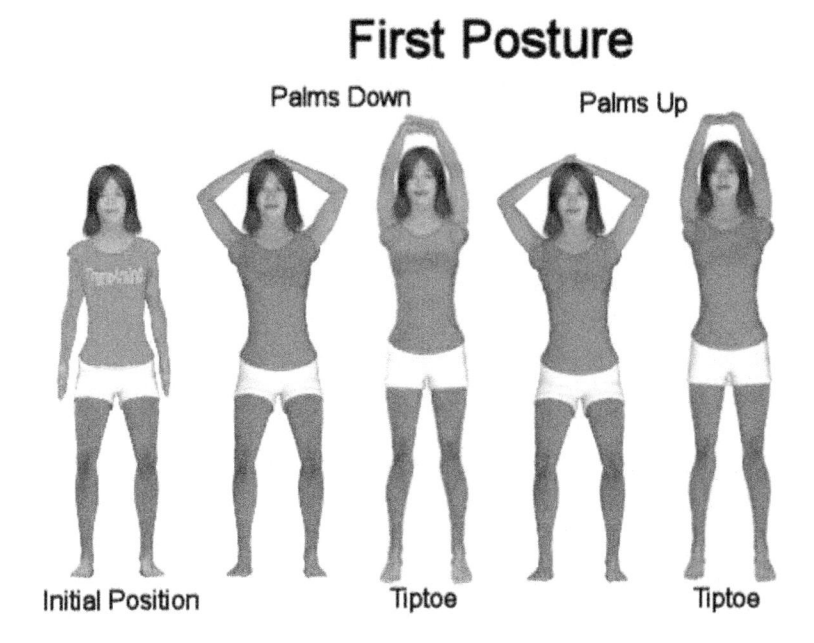

### First Posture

**Palms Down**      **Palms Up**

Initial Position     Tiptoe     Tiptoe

Begin, as always in the Initial Position

1. Swing the arms outwards and place the hands on the head, palms down.
2. Raise the arms above the head, palms facing downwards, and rise on tiptoe, if you are able.
3. Bring the arms down, placing the hands on the head, palms still down. If you stood on tiptoe, stand flat on the floor.
4. Raise the arms, turning them so the palms face upwards

Lower the arms so the hands rest on the head, palms still upwards. Swing the arms down so you are in the Initial Position.

Repeat the whole sequence of actions three or more times.

## *2 Drawing the Bow*

**Set 2 Sequence**

Repeat this sequence three or more times by returning to the starting position and alternating the arms; that is, if you began with the right arm, begin the next sequence beginning with the left arm.

From the Initial Position:
1. Draw up the fists and place them back-of-hand to back-of-hand.
2. Swing out the right fist to the right, and withdraw the left fist, as shown in the picture Position 2 above, as if drawing a bow.
3. Return to the starting position, Position 3, with the fists back-to-back.
4. Swing out the left hand and draw back the right, as if drawing a bow, Position 4 (mirror image of Position 2).

Repeat the sequence two or three times, or more as you progress.

## 3 Raise Each Arm

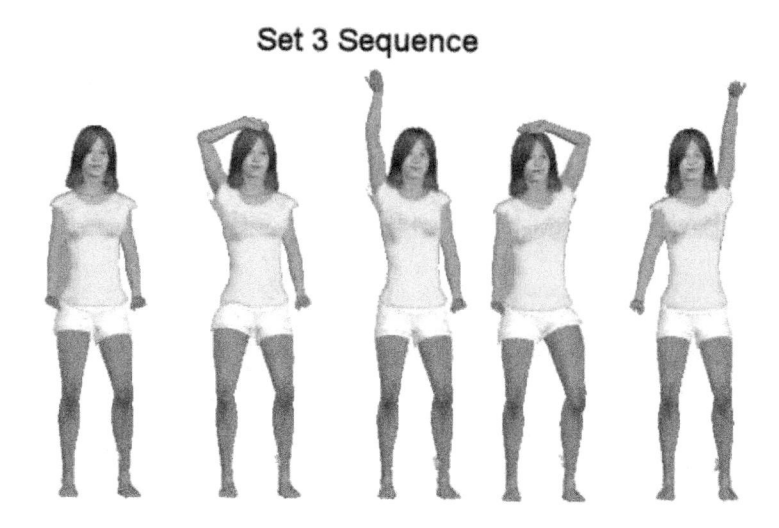

**Set 3 Sequence**

1. From the Initial Position (not shown) turn the hands palms down and press gently down.
2. Raise the right arm and place the hand on the head, palm up. Raise the right arm from the head pushing up with the right hand against an imaginary force, and down with the left hand against an imaginary force.
3. Bring the right hand down and press against an imaginary force as the left hand rises and is placed on the head, palm up.
4. Raise the left hand and press against an imaginary force, while the right hand presses down on an imaginary force.

Perform the set three times (or more if you can).

## *4 Looking Behind*

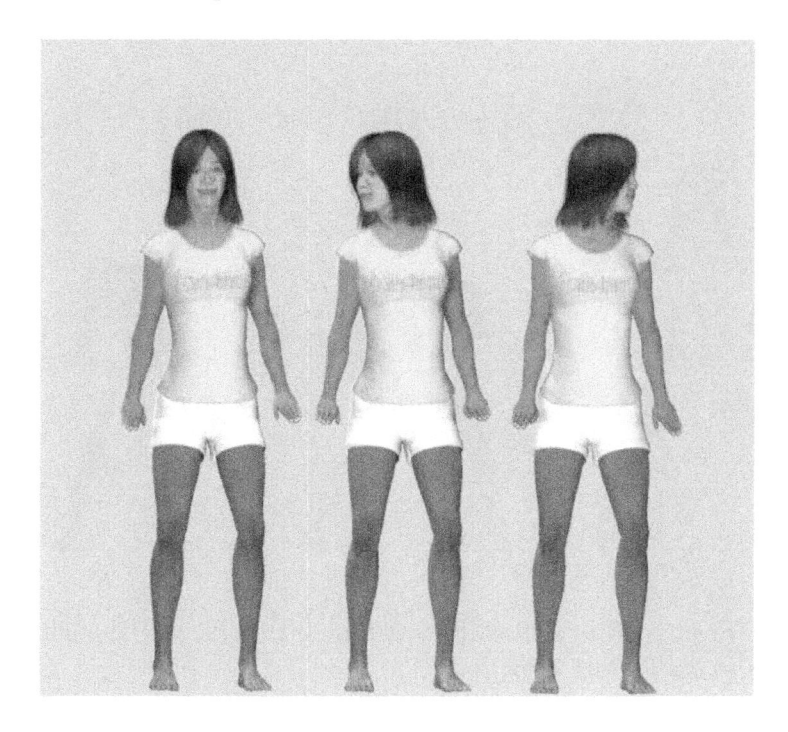

1. From the Initial Position, press down with the hands as if pressing against an imaginary force. (Position 1)
2. Turn the head to the right as far as comfortable. (Position 2)
3. Turn the head to the left as far as comfortable. (Position 3)

Repeat three or more times as comfortable.

# 5 Bending Over and Wagging the Tail

Set 5 Sequence

1. From the Initial Position, assume the 'horse riding stance', as in the Picture, Position 1.
2. In a circular manner, move the upper body down and to right, and around to the left, and still in a circle return to the starting position.
3. (This is a mirror image of Position 2) In a circular manner, move the upper body down and to left, and around to the right, and still in a circle return to the starting position.

Repeat the set two or three times (or more if you are able).

71

## 6 *Reaching Down*

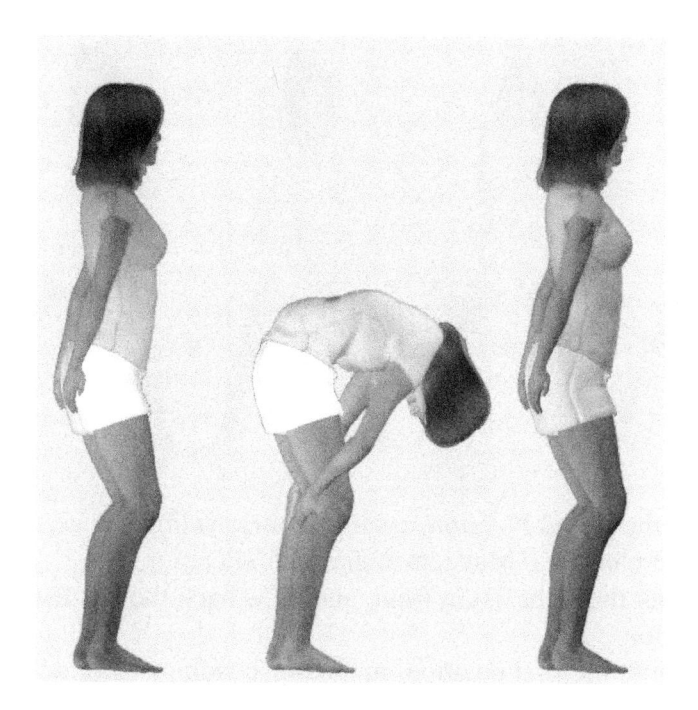

1. From the Initial Position, place your hands on the buttocks. ([Position 1](Position 1))
2. Slowly bend down, running the hands down the backs of the legs, as far as you can easily. ([Position 2](Position 2))
3. Return to the starting position, running your hands along the legs until you reach the first position. ([Position1](Position1))

Repeat the set two or three times (or more).

## 7 Punching With Angry Gaze

1. From the Initial Position, assume a horse-riding stance, with the fist clenched. Make an angry face. ([Position 1](#))
2. Roll out the right fist in front, and draw back the left fist. ([Position 2](#).)
3. Return to the first position, in the horse-riding stand, with clenched fists. ([Position 1](#))
4. Roll out the left fist in front, and draw back the right fist. ([Position 3](#).)

Repeat three or more times.

## *8 Touch the Toes*

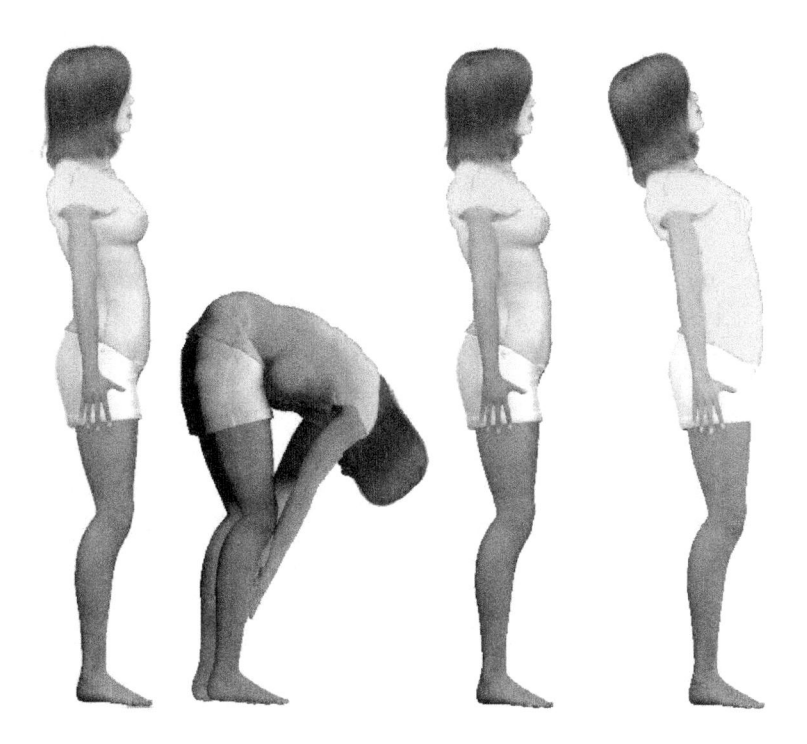

1. From the Initial Position, bend down, brushing the fronts of the legs with the hands. Go down as far as is comfortable. Some can place their hands flat on the floor, but most cannot. Go as far as you can, while avoiding over-stretching. (Position 1)
2. Return to the Initial Position, and bend backwards as far as is comfortable. (Position 2)

Repeat two or three times (or more if you can)

Printed in Great Britain
by Amazon